SHIT BOMBS FOR ASSHOLES

SWEAR WORD COLORING BOOK

Kate Blume
blumesberry art

S
Page Addie Press

ISBN: 978-0-6480768-2-7 paperback.
BIC Subject category: 1. Arts & Photography. 2. Drawing-coloring books for grown-ups
3. Craft, hobbies 4. Self-help-art therapy & relaxation 5. Self-help-anger management

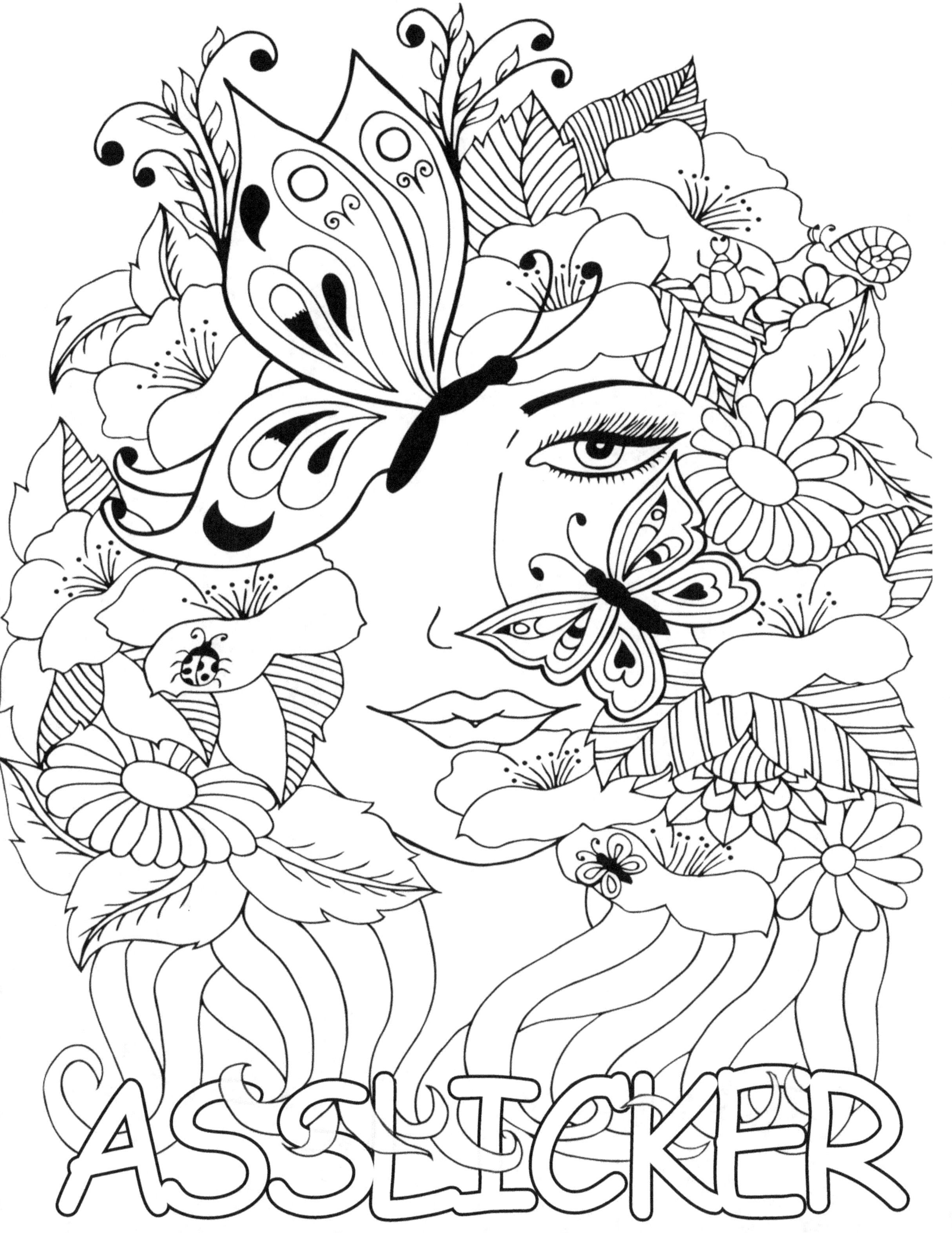
ASSLICKER

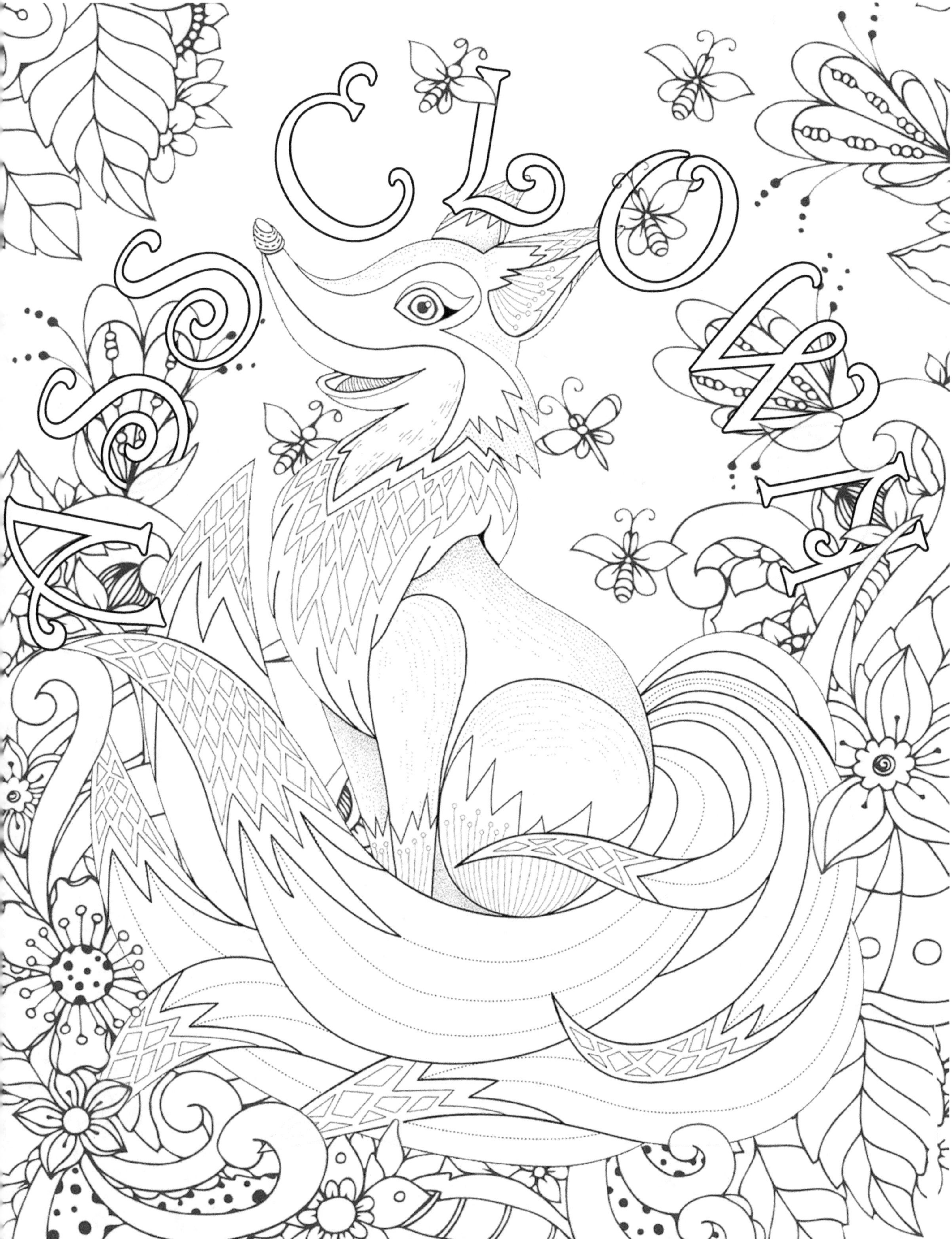

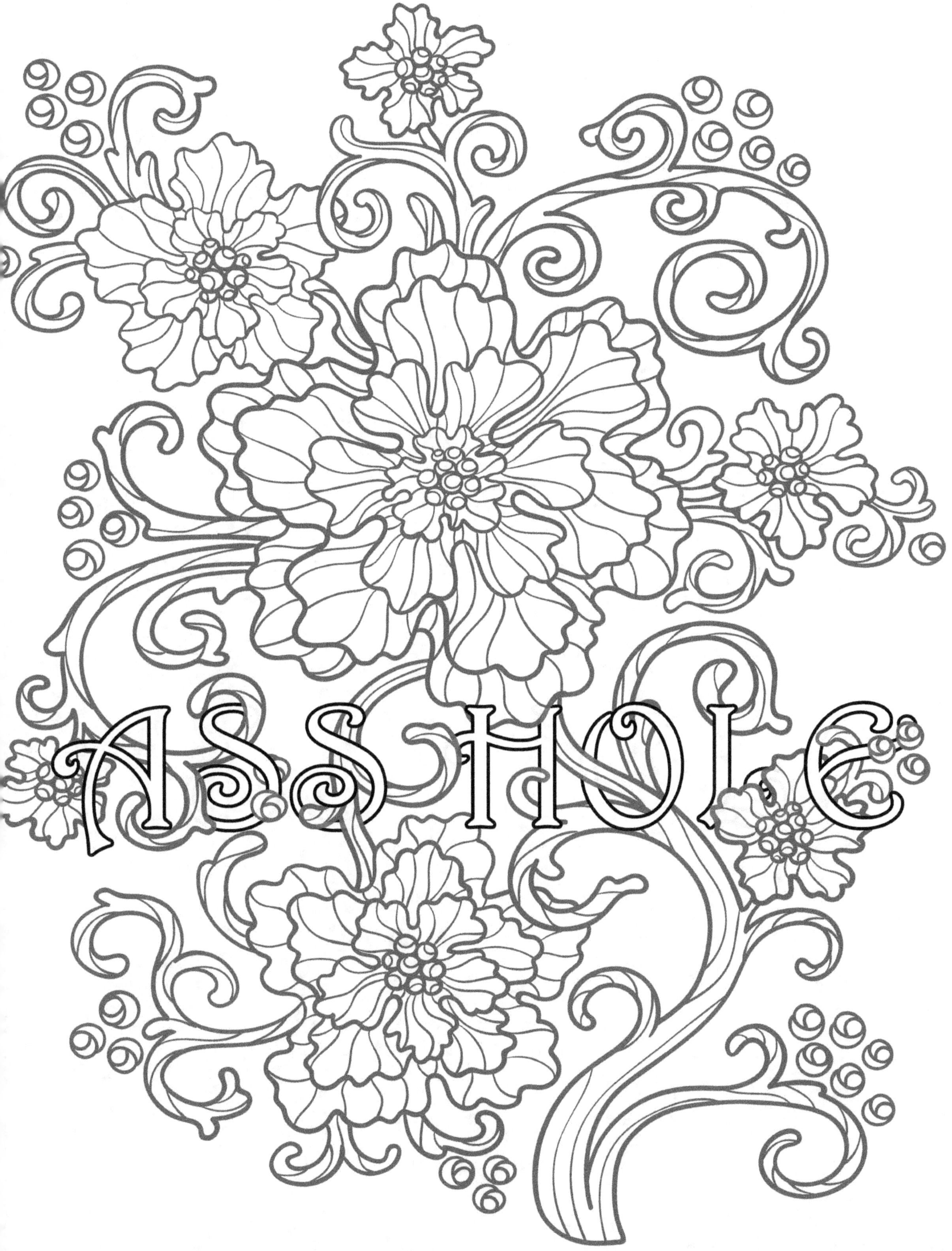
ASSHOLE

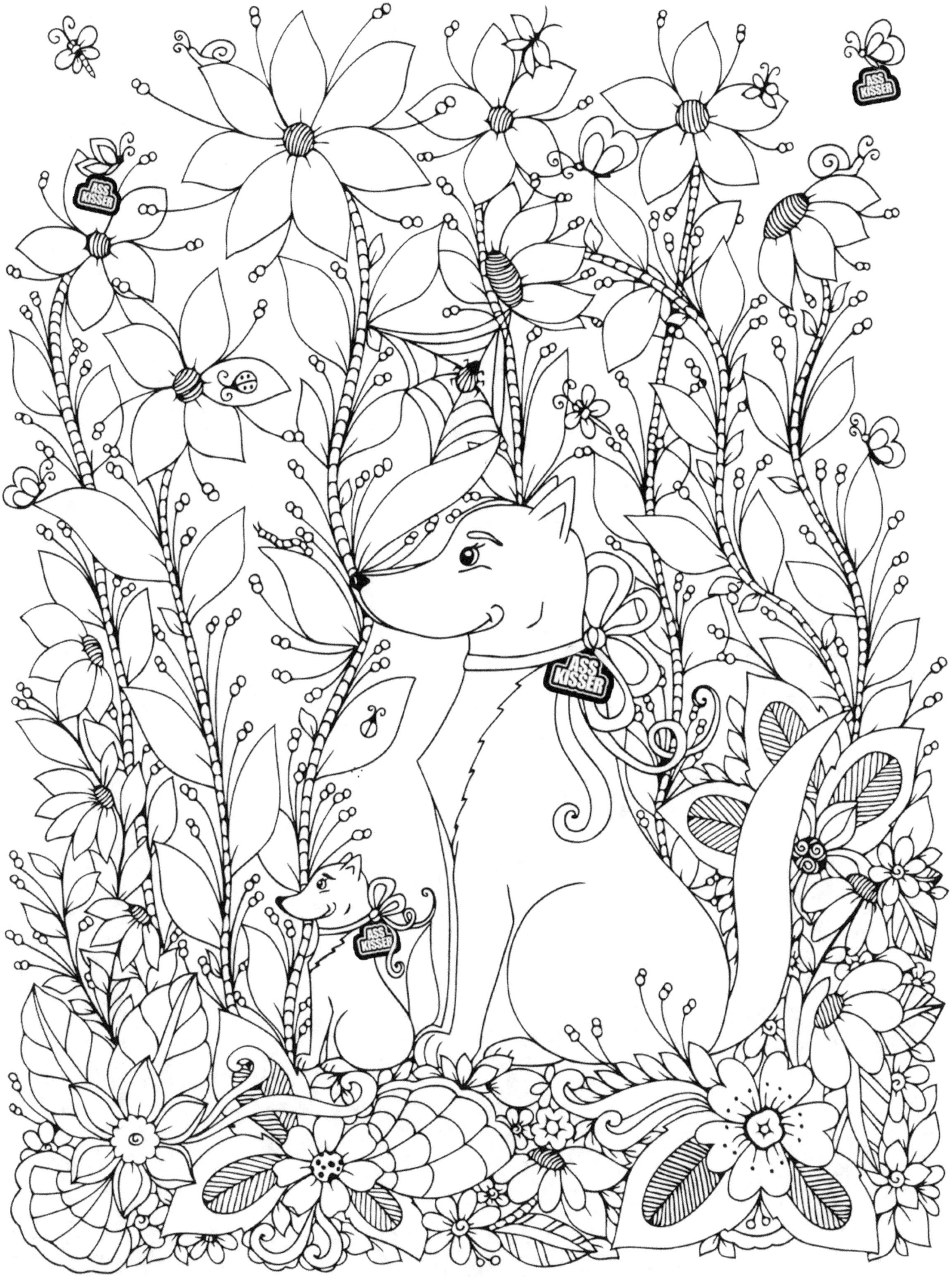
ASS KISSER
ASS KISSER
ASS KISSER
ASS KISSER

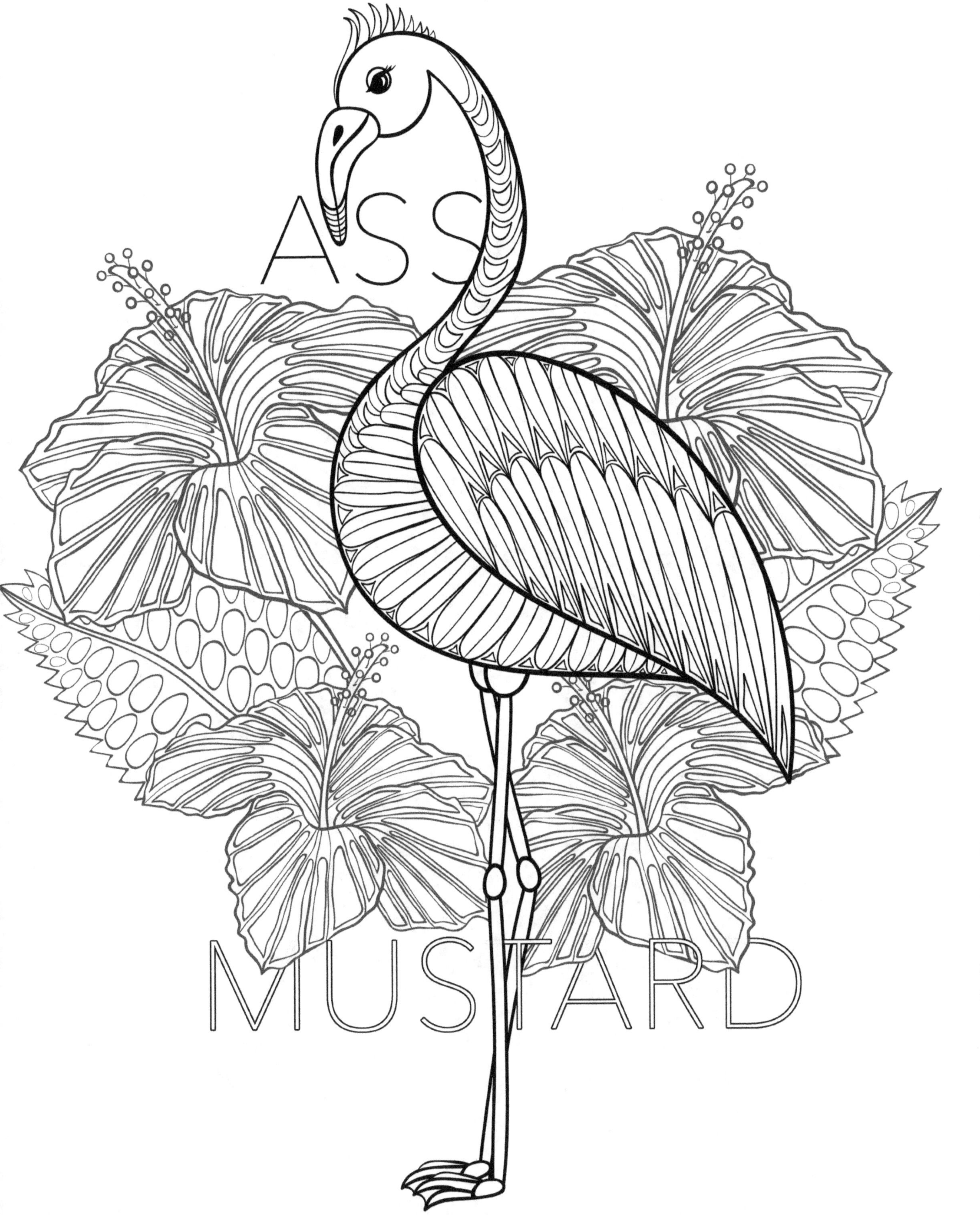
ASS
MUSTARD

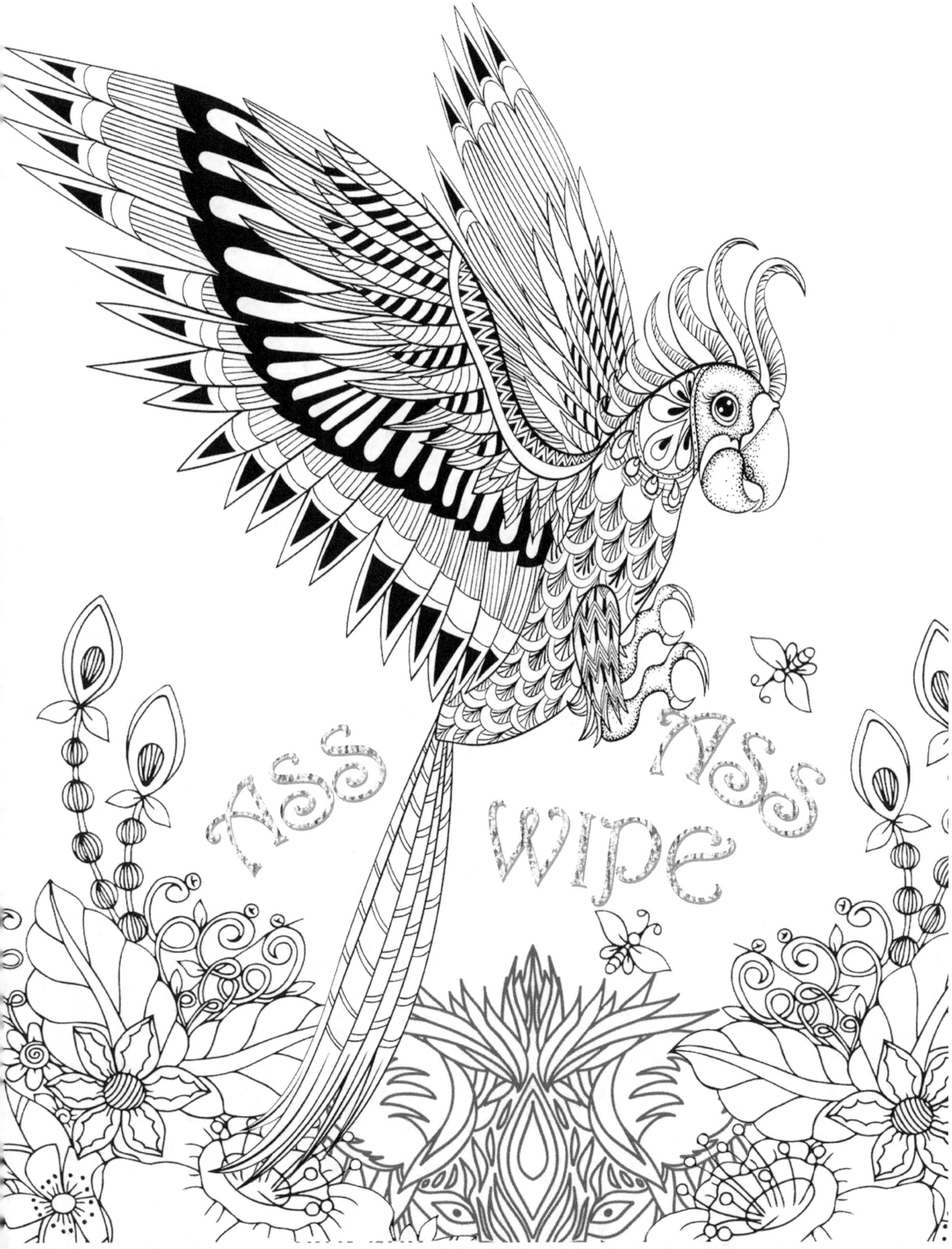
Ass
Wipe

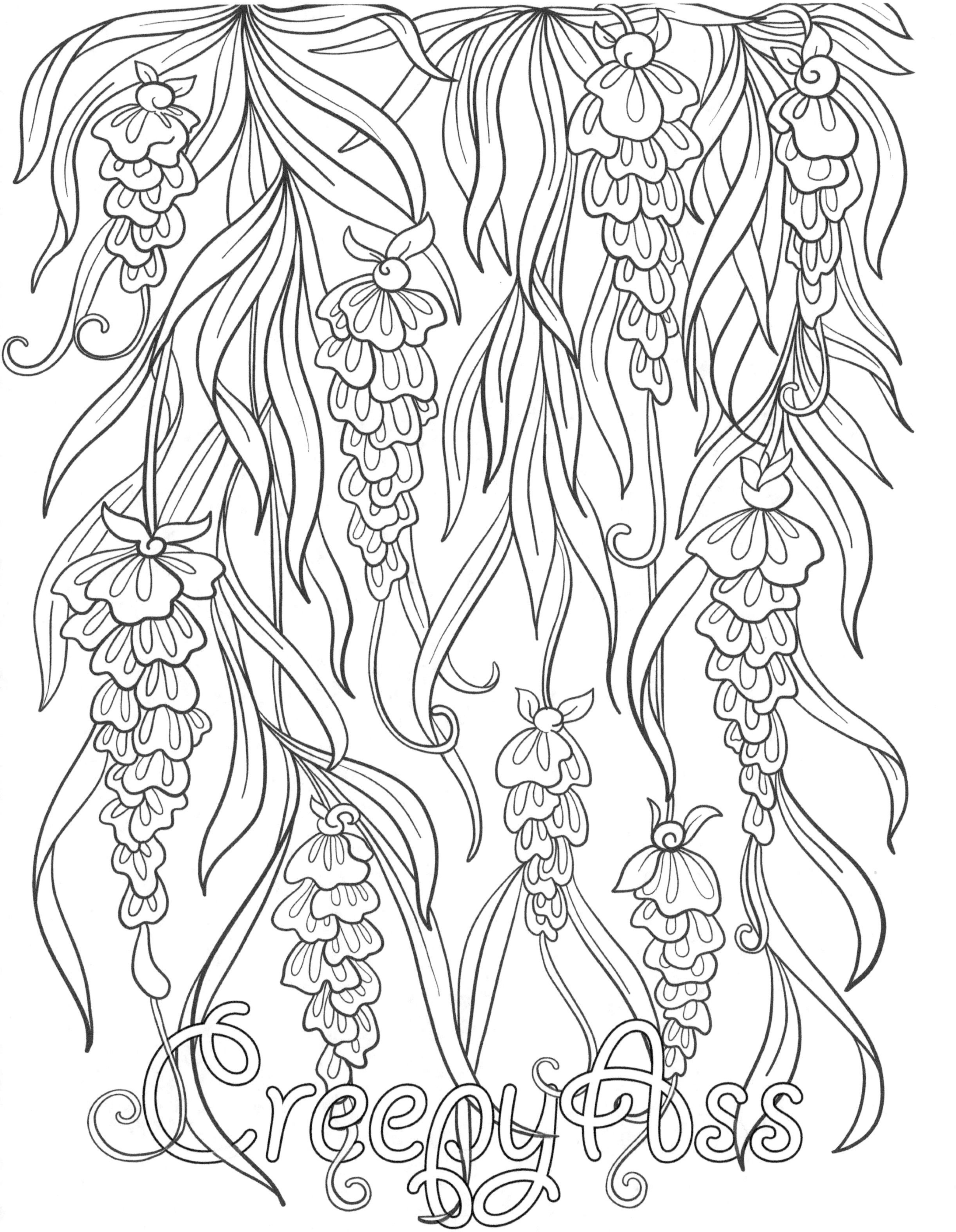
Creepy Ass

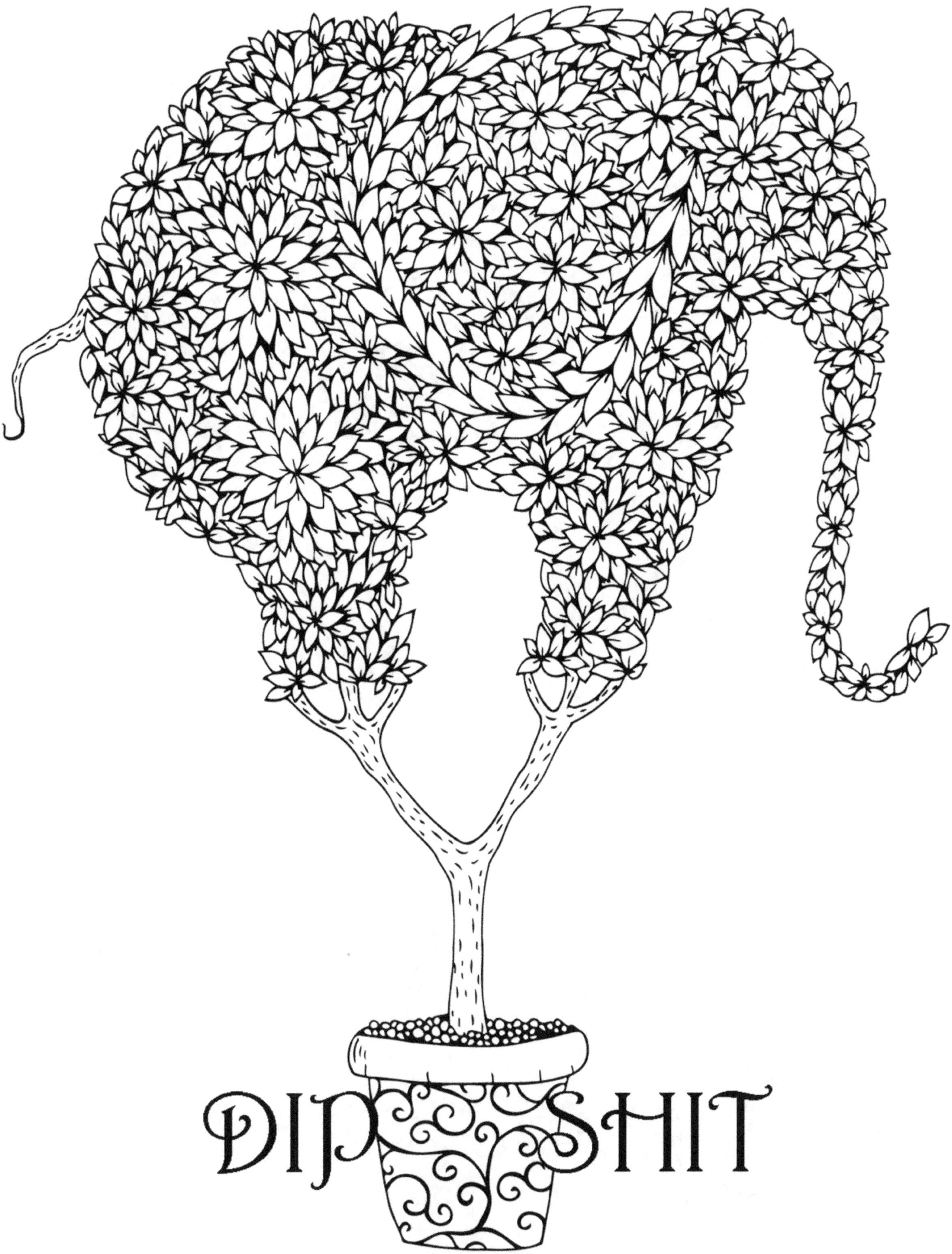
DIP SHIT

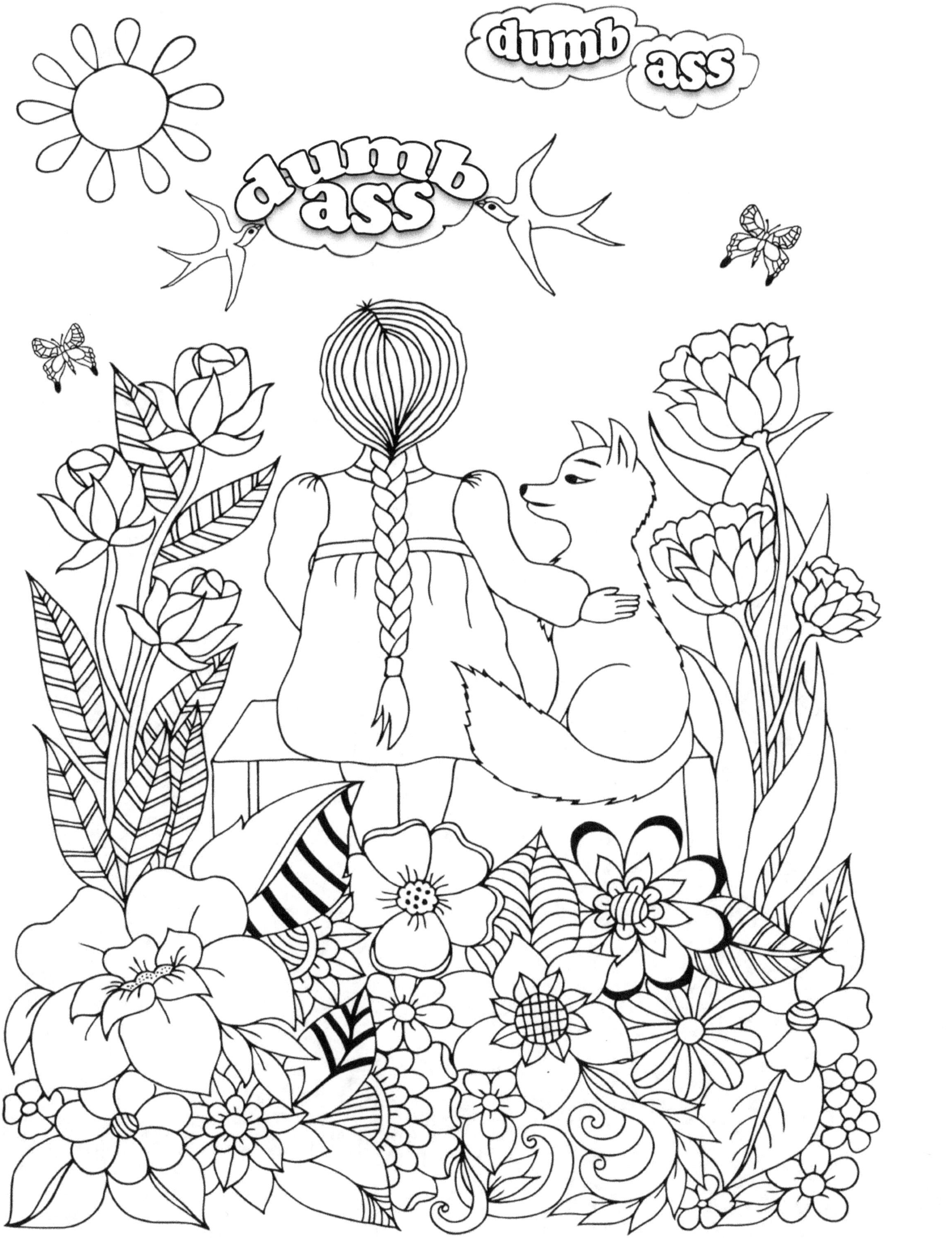
dumb ass
dumb ass

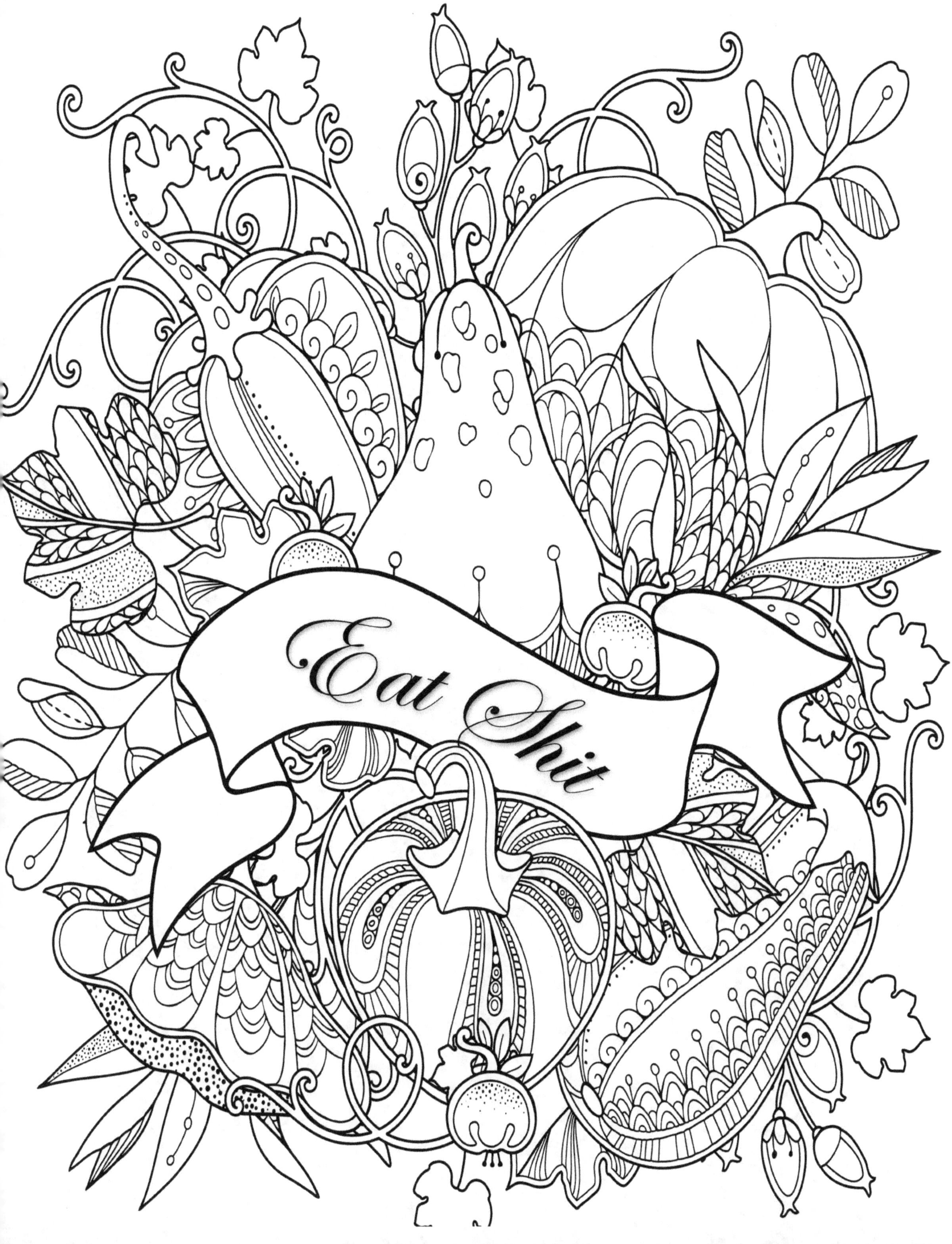
Eat Shit

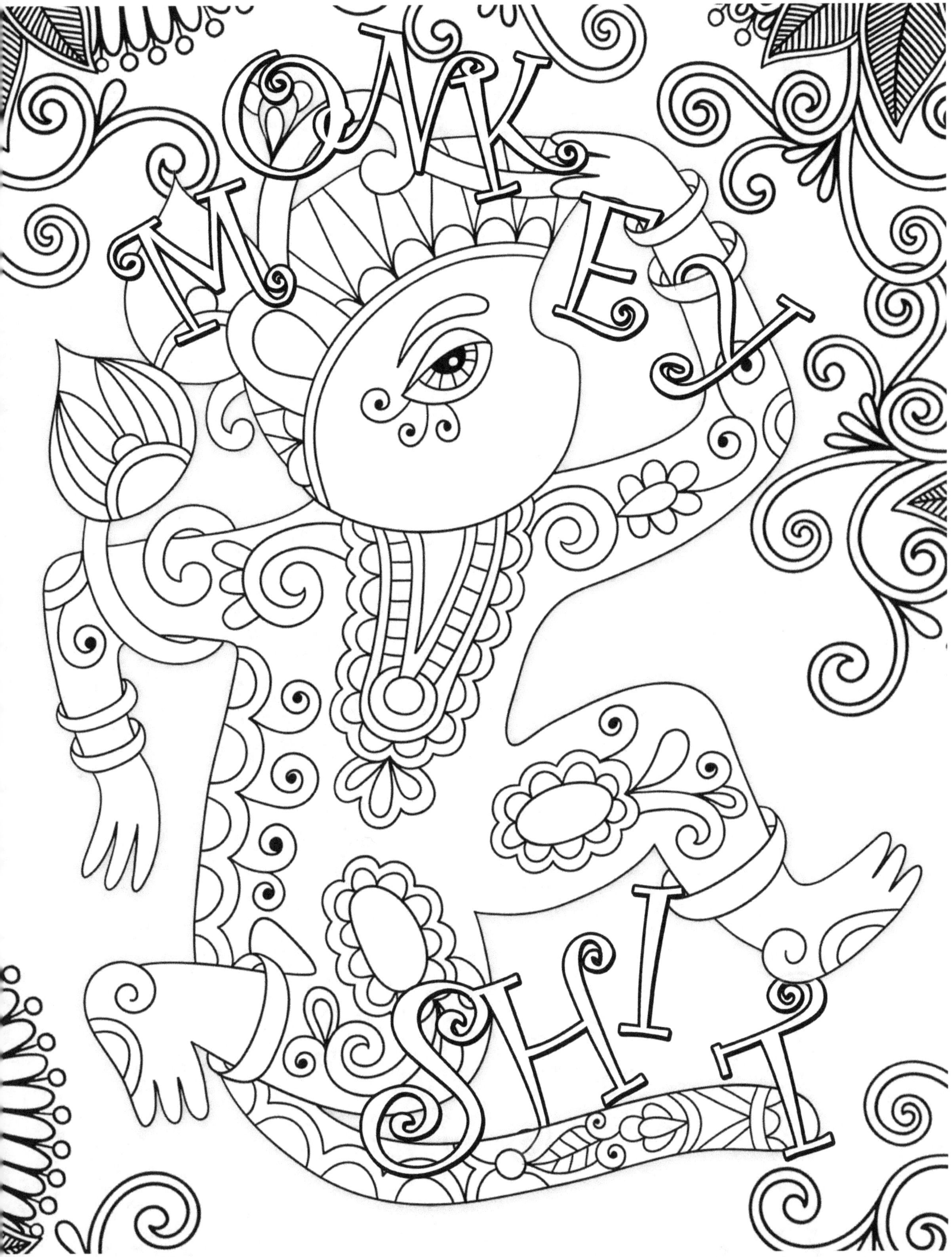
MONKEY
SHIT

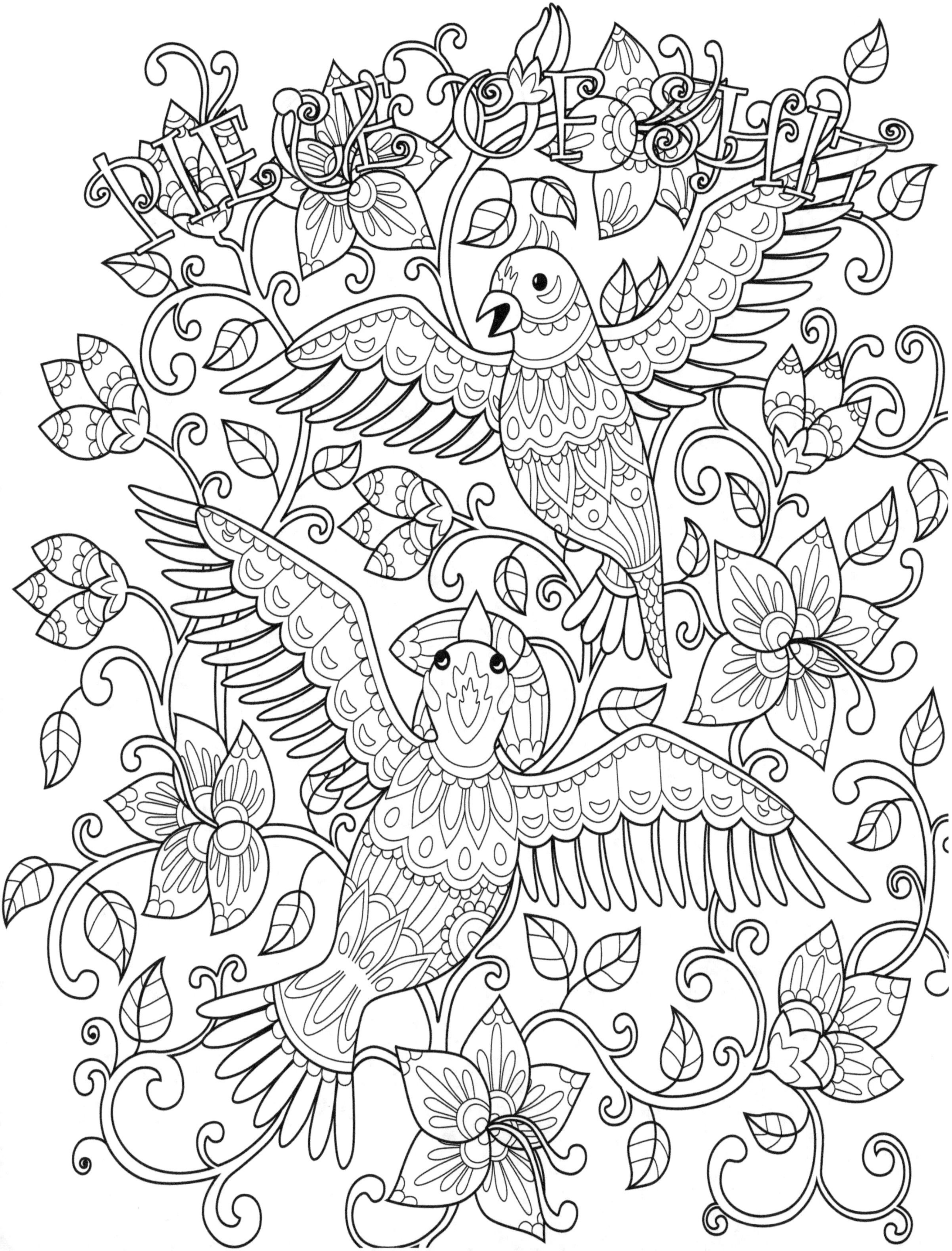
PIECE OF SHIT

RECTAL TREMBLER

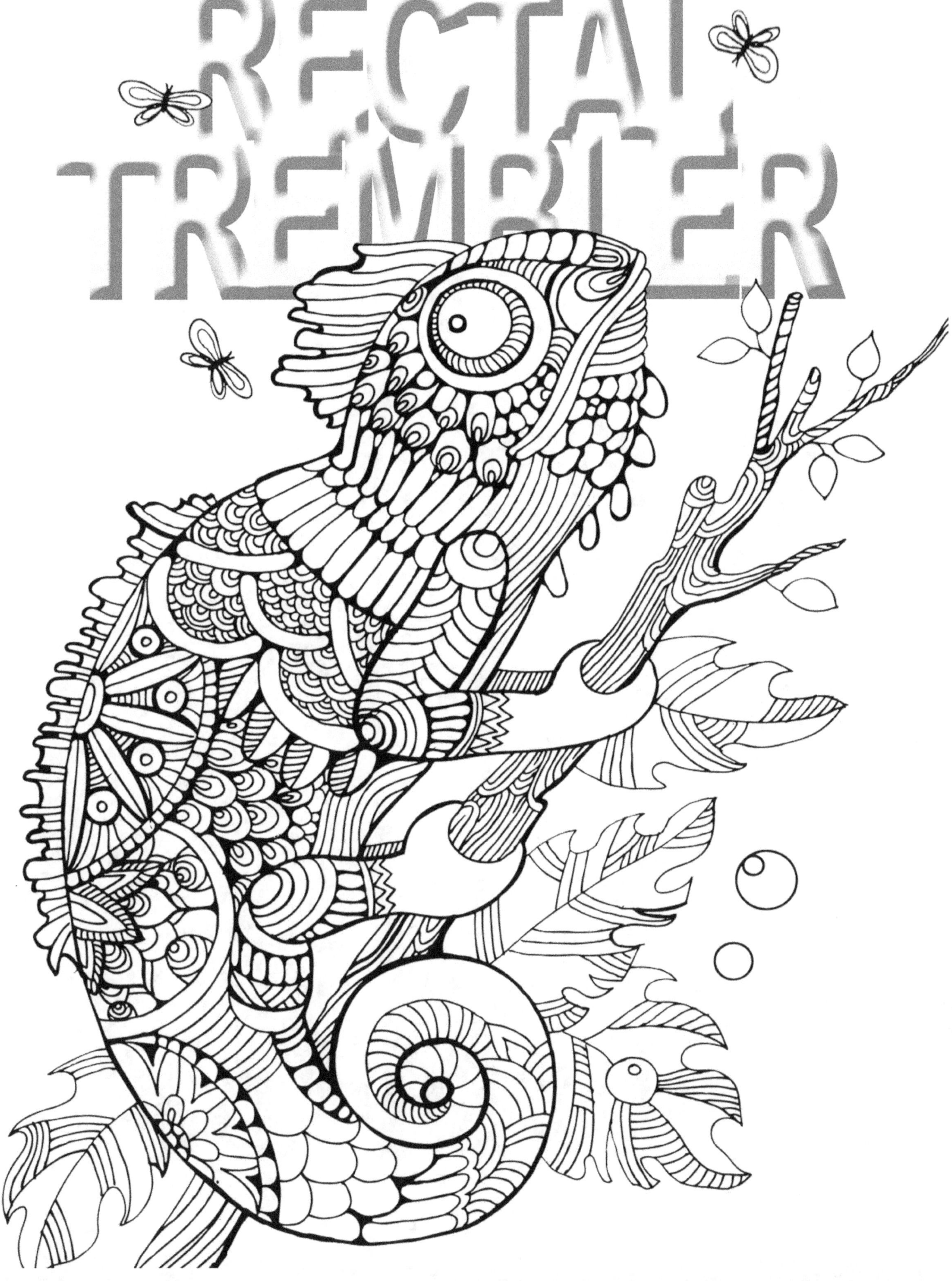

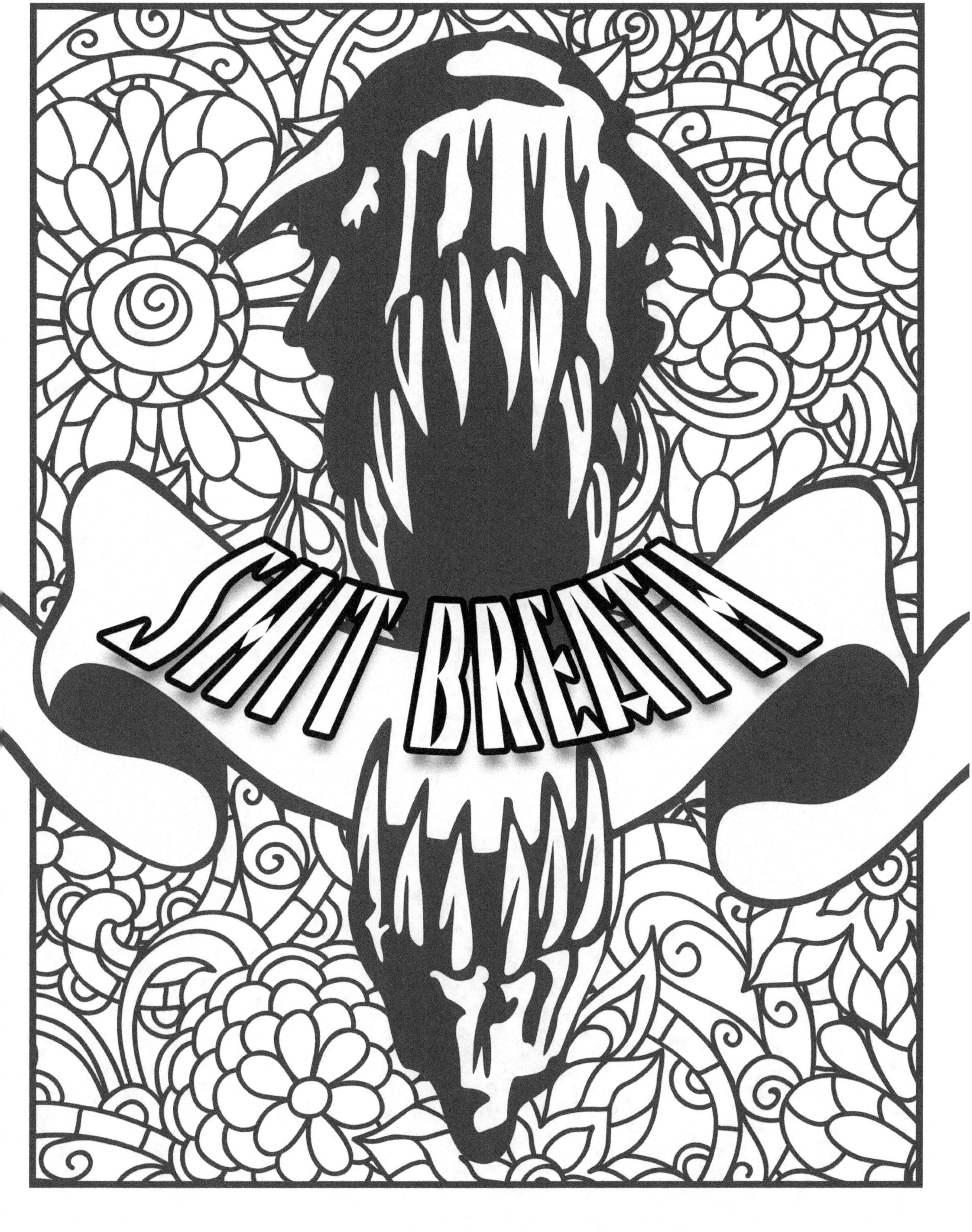
SHIT BREATH

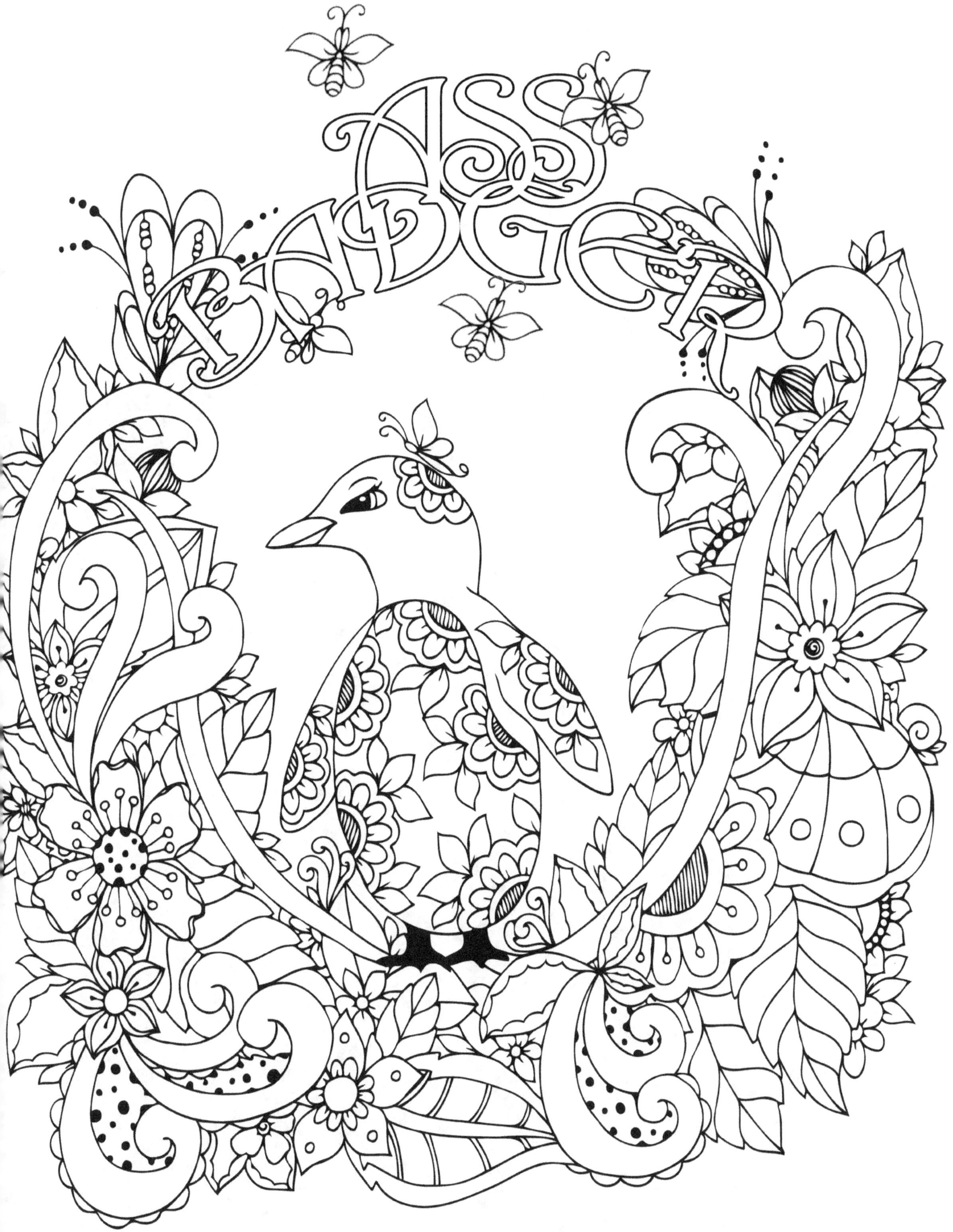
ASS
BADGER

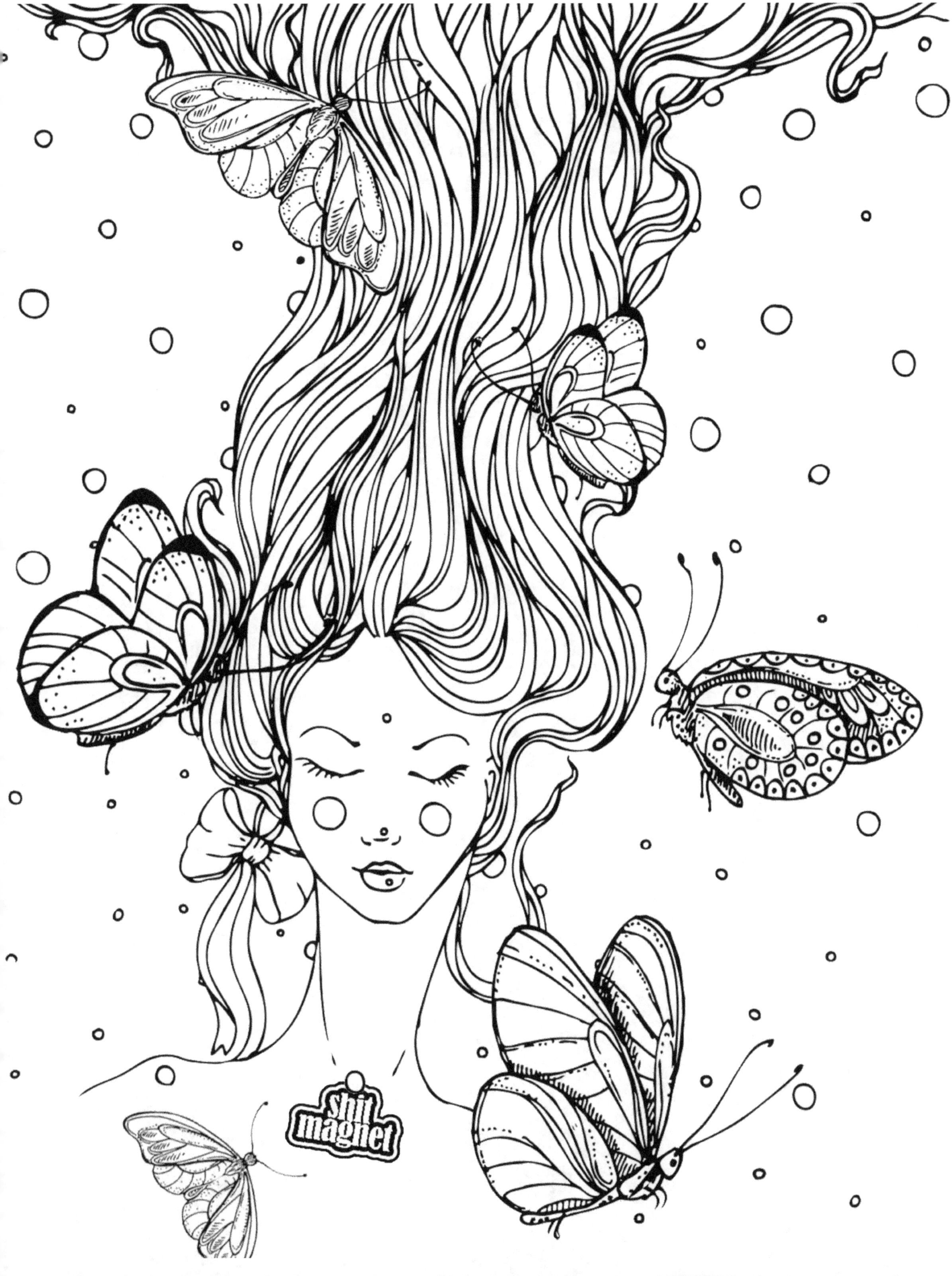
shit magnet

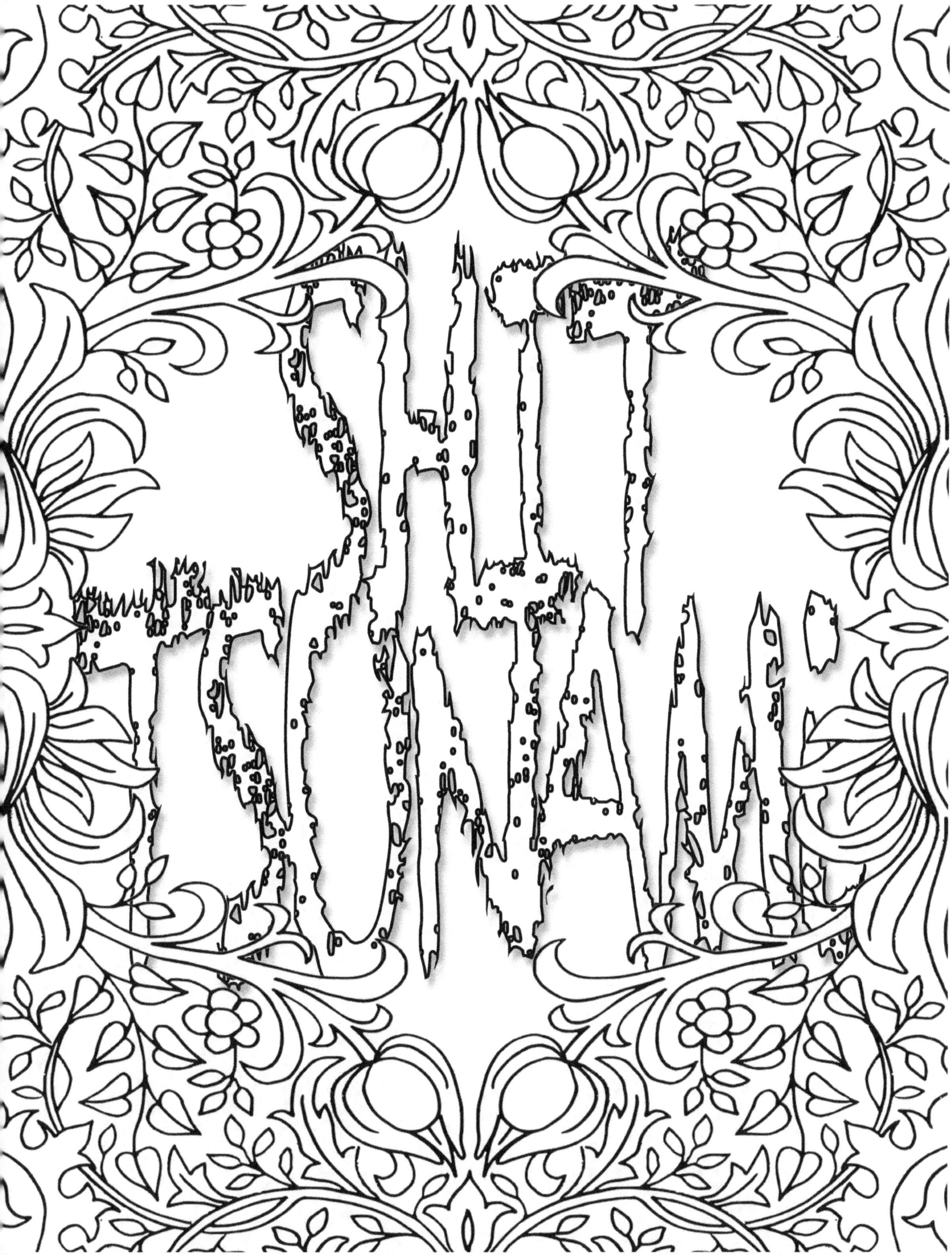
SHIT
TSUNAMI!

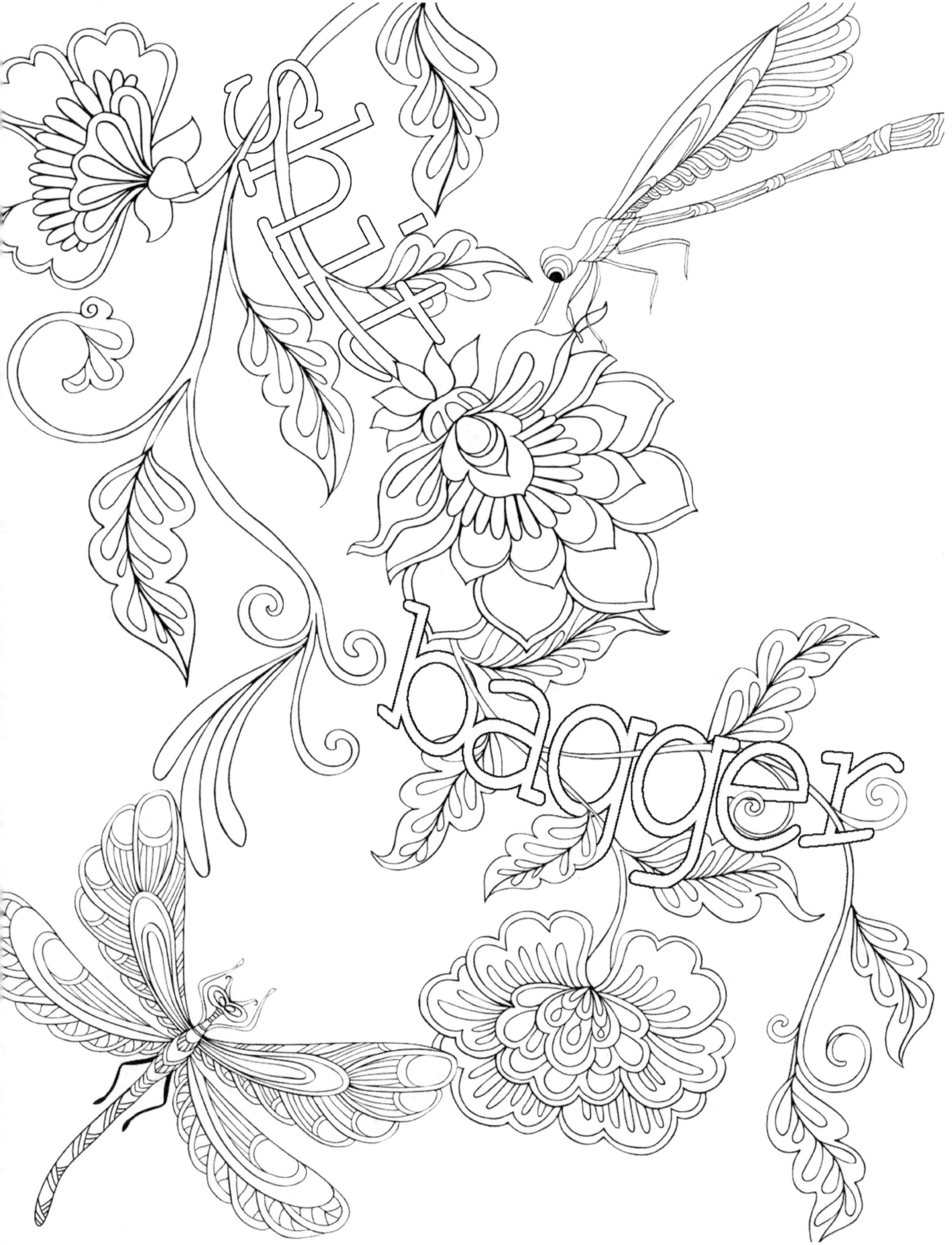
Shift
bagger

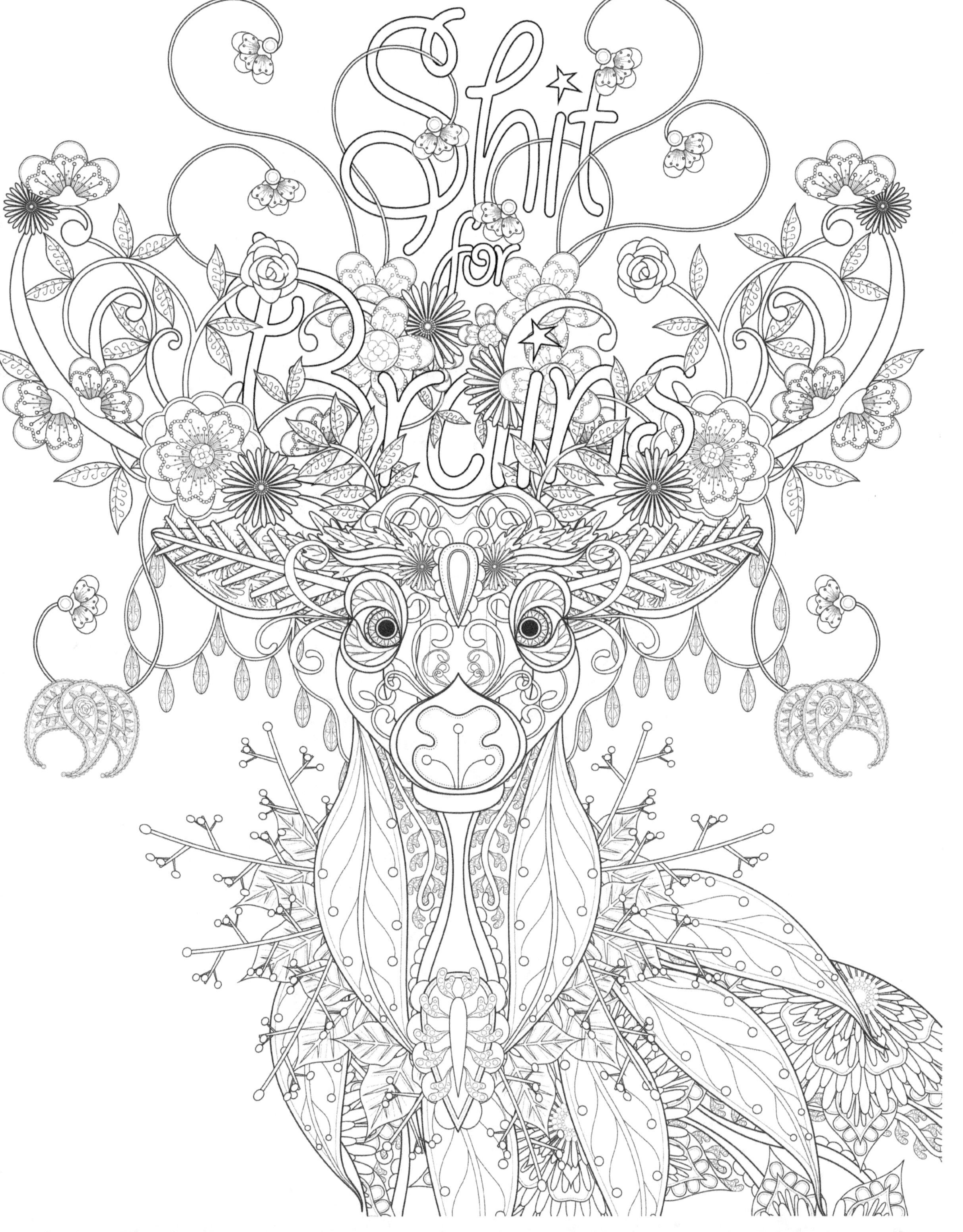
Shit
for
Brains

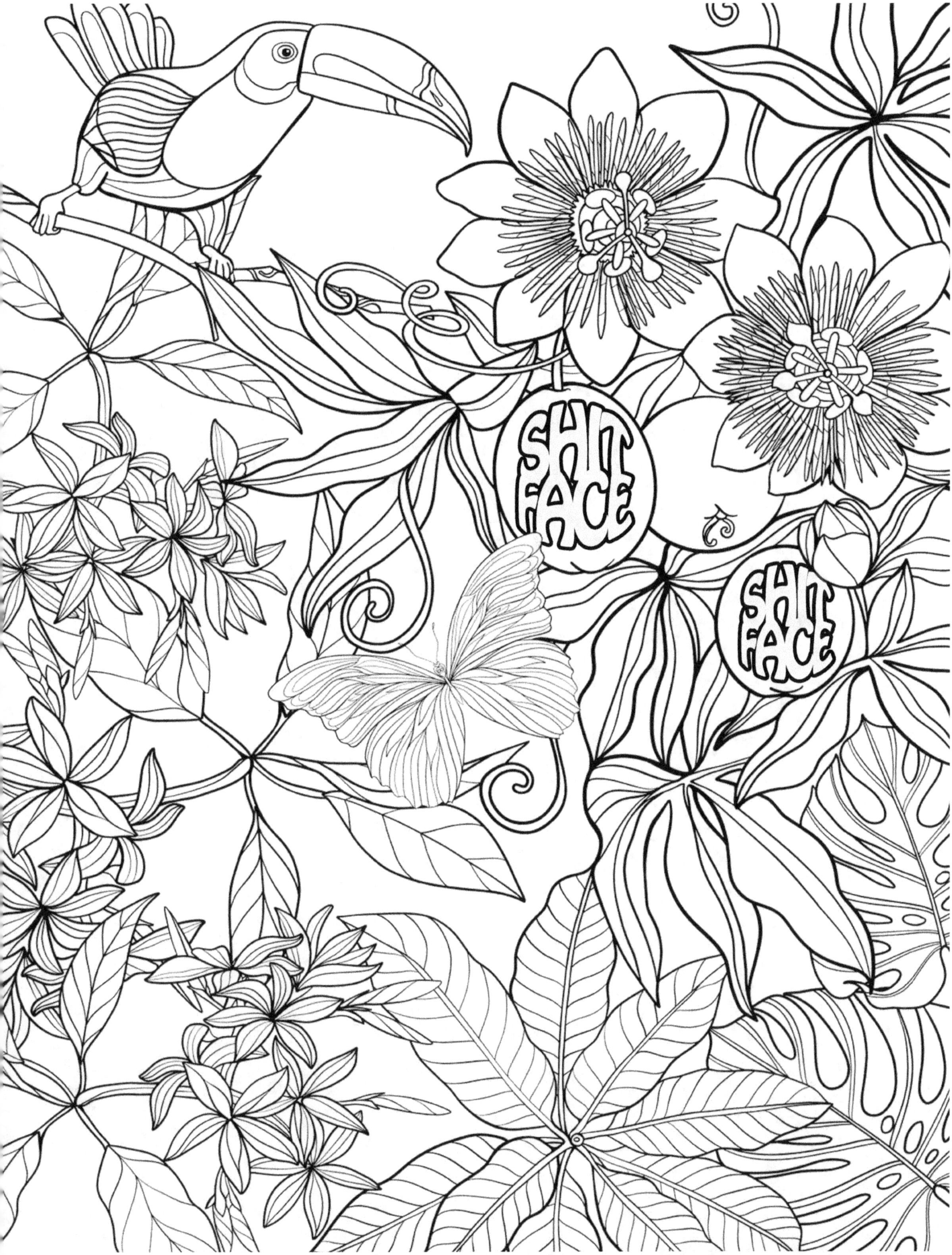
SHIT FACE
SHIT FACE

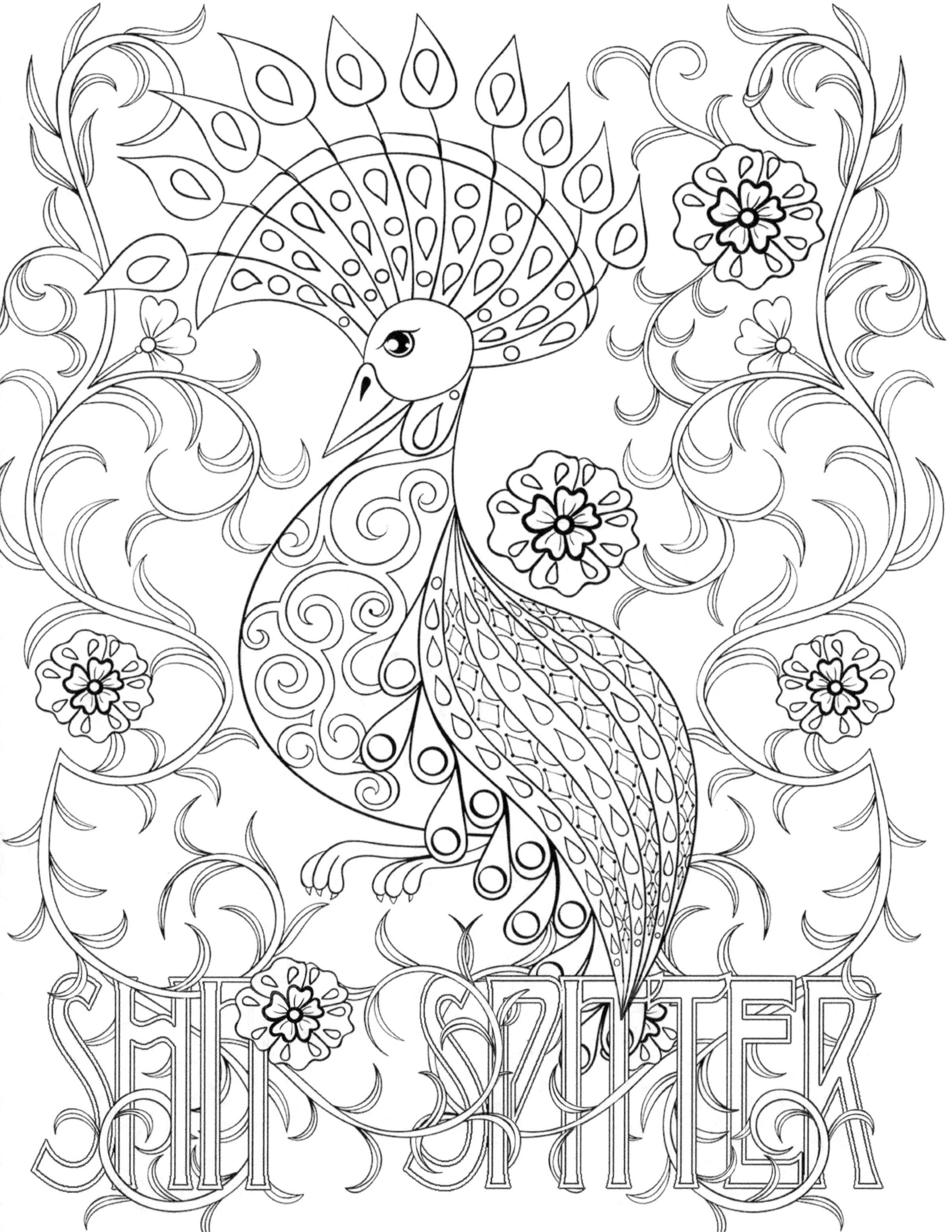
SHIT SPITTER

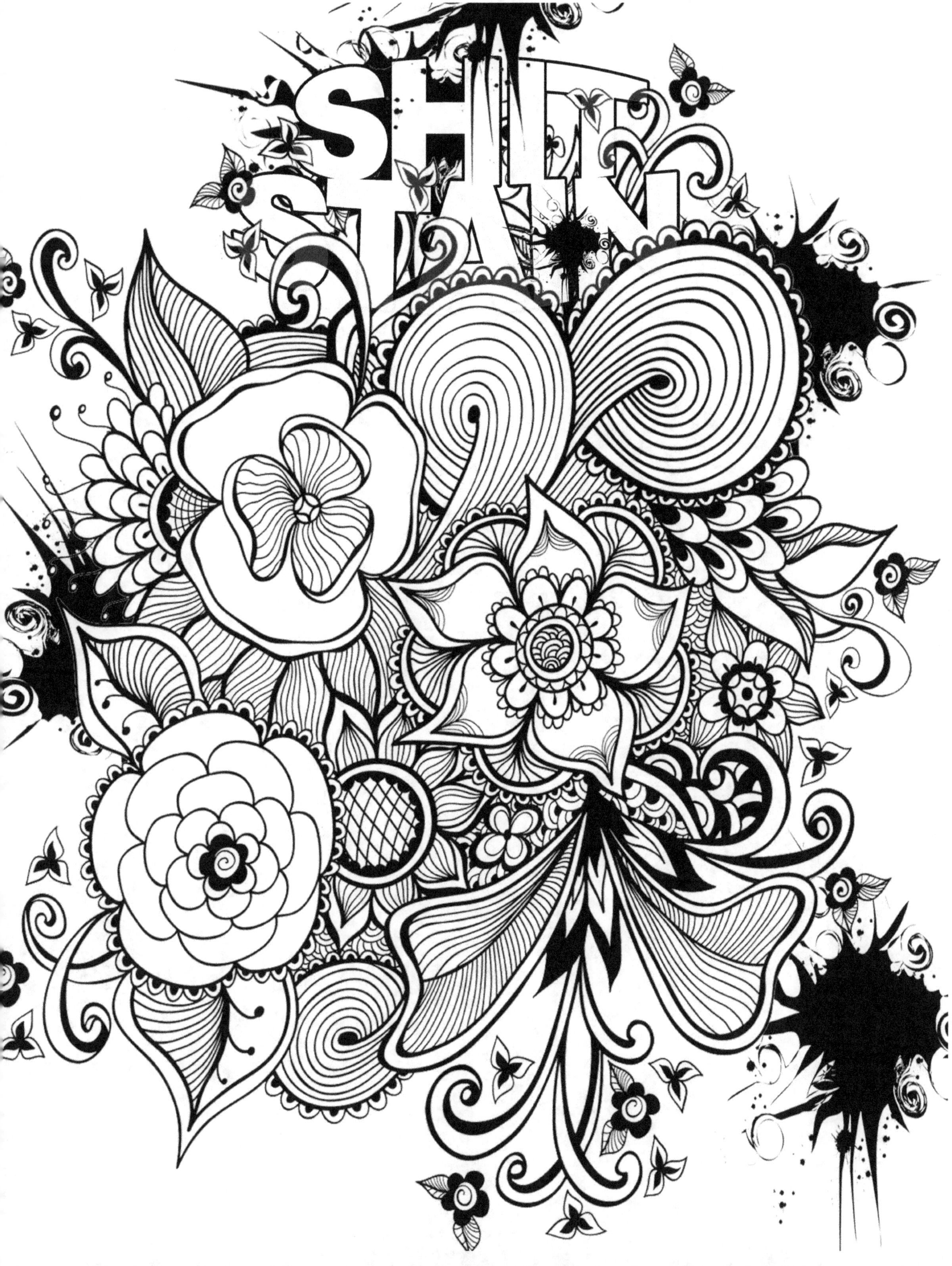
SHIT
STAIN

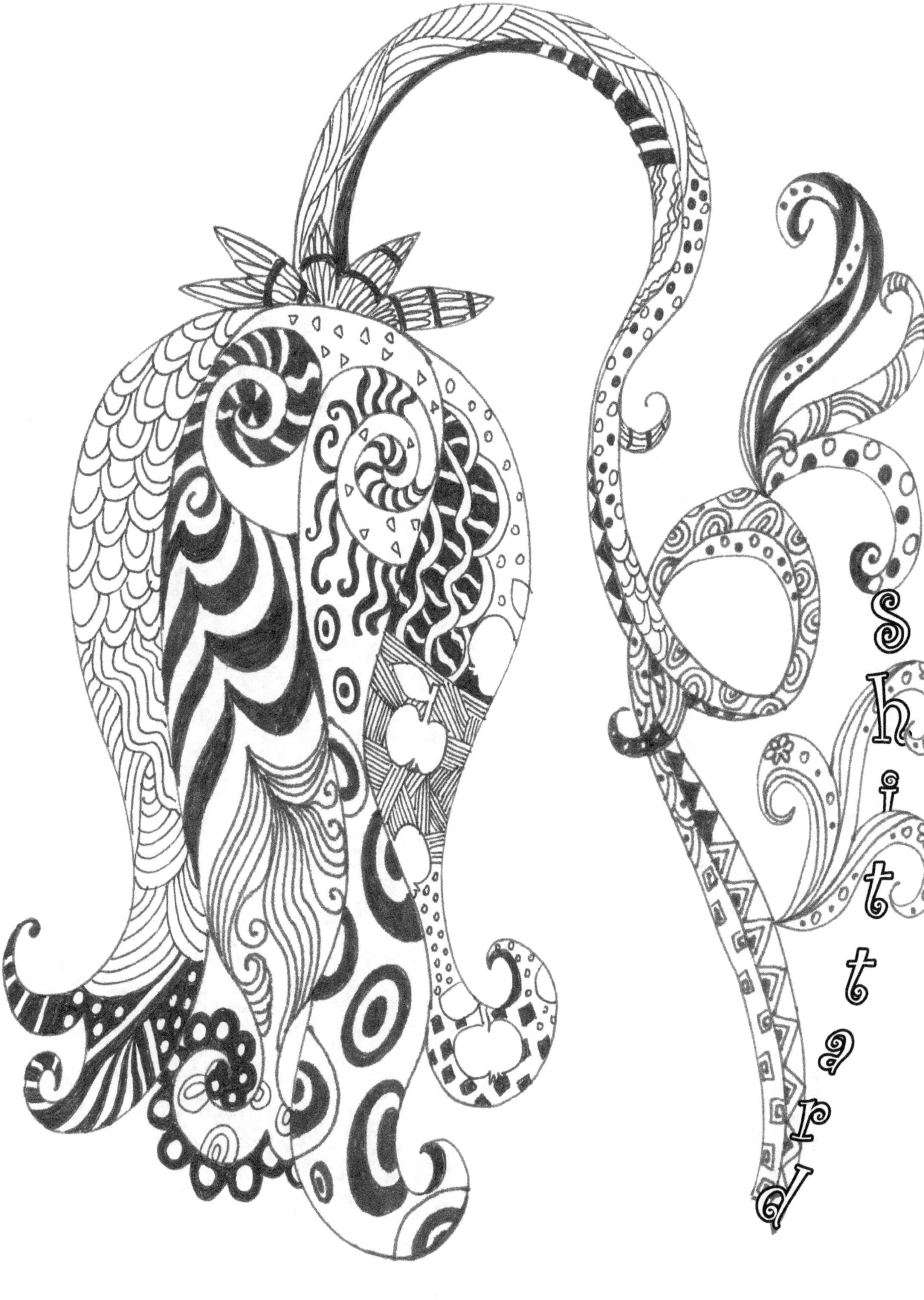
shittard

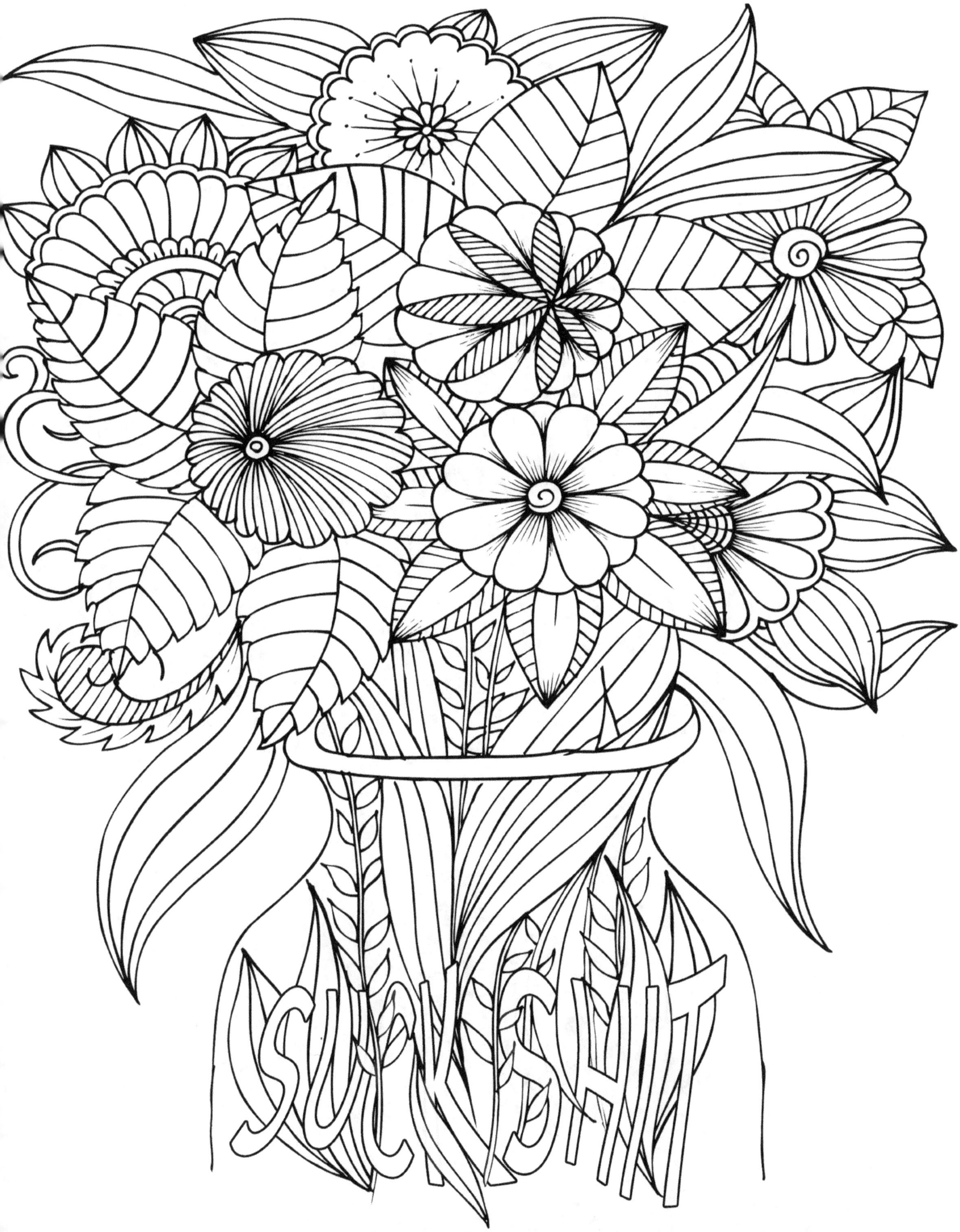
SUCK SHIT

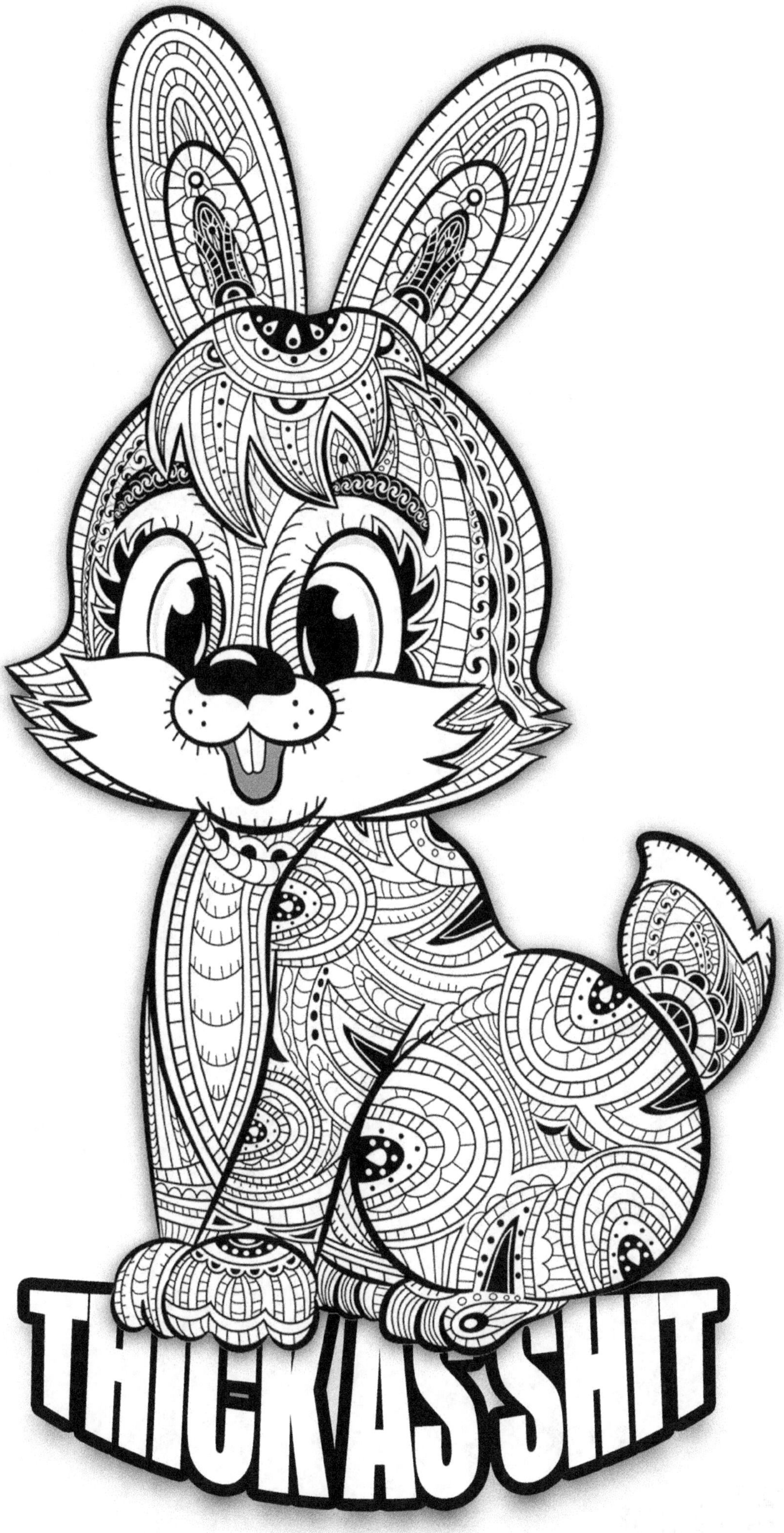
THICK AS SHIT

www.ingramcontent.com/pod-product-compliance
Lightning Source LLC
Chambersburg PA
CBHW080847170526
45158CB00009B/2659
9780648076827